# Cooking Supper

A Division of The **McGraw·Hill** Companies

Columbus, Ohio

**www.sra4kids.com**

*SRA/McGraw-Hill*

*A Division of The* **McGraw·Hill** *Companies*

Send all inquiries to:
SRA/McGraw-Hill
8787 Orion Place
Columbus, OH 43240-4027

ISBN 0-07-569801-3
    3 4 5 6 7 8 9 DBH 05 04 03 02

The children had no choice.
It was something they could not avoid.
At the Smith home, everyone helped with supper.

Dad flipped a coin.
He pointed to Lester.
"Lester will help me boil corn
and broil hamburgers."

Then he pointed to Kate.
"Kate can make salad dressing
with this oil."

A voice called from the family
room. It was Mom.
"I will make a moist cake,"
she said.

Grammy and Gramps joined the
Smiths for supper.
No one was disappointed.
Everything was tasty.

Grammy and Gramps helped, too.
Grammy put foil on the leftovers so
they would not spoil.
And Gramps put them away.